John Harris

The Cruise of the Cutter and other Peace Poems

John Harris

The Cruise of the Cutter and other Peace Poems

ISBN/EAN: 9783743414617

Manufactured in Europe, USA, Canada, Australia, Japa

Cover: Foto ©Thomas Meinert / pixelio.de

Manufactured and distributed by brebook publishing software
(www.brebook.com)

John Harris

The Cruise of the Cutter and other Peace Poems

THE

CRUISE OF THE CUTTER,

AND OTHER

PEACE POEMS.

BY JOHN HARRIS,

AUTHOR OF "SHAKSPERE'S SHRINE," "DULO," "LAYS FROM
THE MINE," ETC.

"And they shall beat their swords into ploughshares, and their spears into pruning-hooks: nation shall not lift up sword against nation, neither shall they learn war any more."—ISAIAH II. 4.

"Glory to God in the highest, and on earth peace, goodwill toward men."—LUKE II. 14.

LONDON:

PARTRIDGE AND CO., 9, PATERNOSTER ROW.

1872.

TO THE

BARONESS BURDETT COUTTS,

DISTINGUISHED FOR HER LIBERALITY TO THE

WORKING CLASSES,

AND HER CHRISTIAN CONSIDERATION OF

The Toilers of Great Britain,

WHOSE GENEROUS NAME WILL GO DOWN TO POSTERITY

AS THE

BENEFACTRESS OF MANKIND,

THESE PEACE POEMS

ARE, BY PERMISSION, HUMBLY AND RESPECTFULLY

INSCRIBED BY

THE AUTHOR.

FALMOUTH, CORNWALL,
July, 1872.

PREFACE.

THE following simple poems have been written with a desire in the author's heart to spread the principles of Peace, and accelerate in some humble way the desired consummation of the beating of swords into ploughshares, and the spears into pruning-hooks, when men shall *learn* war no more. It is surely the duty of Christians of all denominations, of all colours and of all clans,—making the Bible their guide-book, whose holy utterances are peace on earth and goodwill towards men,—to labour for the spread of this precious truth, when man shall meet his BROTHER everywhere, and the dreadful voice of War shall no more be heard. Believing that there is still a power in song to accomplish much for suffering humanity, he offers these original idyls to the candour of his friends and the public, trusting they may ultimately accomplish the end for which they were written.

Throughout his several preceding volumes of prose and poetry, published between the years 1853 and 1871, the author has feebly raised his voice against the curse of war, as the direst calamity that affects the human race; though this is his first exclusive effort to pourtray the falsity of fighting. Should these rustic pictures, sketched by one who has been a British labourer, above ground and below, for more than forty years, who was impressed with the wickedness of warfare when wandering with his boy-harp amid the heather of his Cornish heights, tend to strengthen the ardour of the disciples of Peace, and incite the young to devote their energies and influence to the spread of its saving doctrines, as inculcated by the Great Teacher Himself, he feels he shall not have written in vain.

It is but right to state that this little work originated with Mr. John Gill, whose efficient labours in various Sunday-schools have enabled him to form Bond of Peace Societies. The local names mentioned in these lyrics are mostly real, and many of the word-paintings are from nature. To the young especially of all households he humbly offers this earnest tribute of Peace.

> " No war, or battle's sound,
>   Was heard the world around :
>   The idle spear and shield were high up-hung ;
>   The hooked chariot stood,
>   Unstained with hostile blood :
>   The trumpet spake not."

1872.

CONTENTS.

PEACE POEMS.

WE WILL EVER BE KIND TO ALL.

WEAKNESS, gentleness and worth,
In the ages of the earth,
Have been left where boasters brawl,
But we'll ever be kind to all.

Should a brother lose his track,
We will strive to lure him back,
Holding up the hands that fall,
For we'll ever be kind to all.

Bird and beast, by steep and strand,
In the ocean, or on the land,
Whether they walk, or whether they crawl,
We will ever be kind to all.

Children playing in the lane,
Driver whistling on the wain,
Travellers great, and travellers small,
We will ever be kind to all.

B

Old and young, and rich and poor,
In the meadow or on the moor,
Until rifles rust and fall,
We will ever be kind to all.

EDDY EAST.

" OPEN the door, mother, quickly,
   Our Eddy is down by the gate,
And, O, he is looking so poorly !
   Be active, and don't let him wait."
And soon on his neck she was sobbing,
   And kissing the face of her son ;
The fire was alight, and the kettle
   Its musical song had begun.

His father came down from the chamber,
   And vowed he would rather behold
His Eddy once more in his cottage
   Than have any measure of gold.
His sister, the beautiful Polly,
   As bright as the forehead of Day,
Was clapping her hands in her gladness,
   And dancing around like a fay.

They put him to rest in the settle :
   Then said, with a sob, the poor boy, —
" I'm come home to stay with you, mother,
   And have done with the soldier's employ.

The fruit of the battle is baleful,
  Unfit for a mortal to see ;
The glory is all in the glitter,
  So the farm and the garden for me."

AN ECHO FROM MOUNT LEBANON.

An echo from Mount Lebanon,
  Amid the cedars grand !
O, spears shall change to pruning-hooks,
  Throughout the peaceful land :
Sharp swords shall into ploughshares turn,
  And fighting days be o'er,
All nations learn the arts of Peace,
  And War shall be no more.

Far down the cycles of the past
  This joyful sound has come,
It rings throughout the palace vast,
  In every poor man's home :
'Tis heard along the lonely wood,
  In ocean's solemn roar,
And spreads from listening vale to vale,
  That War shall be no more.

The palms, where Israel's prophets trod,
  Still murmur on the plain,
And prince and peasant lift their heads
  To catch the silvery strain.

B 2

From Cedron's brook to Carmel's crest,
　From Hor to Albion's shore,
From east to west, from north to south,
　That War shall be no more.

O this belief shall still be ours,
　In spite of spear and shield,
And fighting ships, and fighting men;
　We cannot, dare not yield.
The beams of Peace will shortly break
　Through Morning's golden door,
And stream on all the gladdened earth,
　And War shall be no more.

THE LAST STICK.

" BRING forth the last stick, Marie,
　And lay it on the brands:
The wintry winds are roaring
　Along the barren sands.
The sleet is cold and cruel
　That driveth down the hill,
And beateth on the casement;
　But man is harder still.

" Bring forth the last stick, Marie,
　And draw your cricket nigh
While the weak pottage cooketh,
　That we may eat and die.

There's nothing more to cheer us,
    From cupboard, shelf or chest:
We'll say our prayers together,
    And look to Heaven for rest.

" Bring forth the last stick, Marie;
    Your sire will come no more;
Your brother with him lieth,
    Where earth is red with gore.
What darkness and what anguish
    The war has forced us through!
Bring forth the last stick, Marie,
    'Tis all that we can do."

THE STRONG SMITH BY THE SEA.

In the peaceful days to be,
Worked a strong smith by the sea,
Chanting thus, with bosom bare,
" The sword I change to the shining share."

Heaps of spears in his smithy lay,
Blades gore-dyed in the fearful fray,
And the sparks rose high on the balmy air,
As the sword was changed to the shining share.

And loud the monster bellows roared,
Redd'ning many an ancient sword:
" This is the way," sang the strong smith there,
" To change the spear to the shining share."

The great wind came from the northern moor
And shook the walls from roof to floor,
But that steady smith, in the forge's glare,
Still changed the sword to the shining share.

And ever that strong man laboured he,
Summer and winter, beside the sea,
With heavy hammer and bosom bare,
Till the swords were changed to the shining share.

A CHILD GREW UP AT NAZARETH.

A CHILD grew up at Nazareth,
   The Infinite made man,
Who, self-existent, long had reigned
   Before the stars began.
He spoke by Cedron's flowing brook
   With lips that cannot lie,
" Whoever takes the sword of war
   Shall fall himself thereby."

Men heard it, but they heeded not,
   And turned their ears away,
Snatched up in ire the battle-axe
   And perished in the fray.
Yet still the echo rolleth on,
   And filleth earth and sky,
" Whoever takes the sword of war
   Shall fall himself thereby."

And as the centuries come and go
    They oft this fact proclaim,
Where hostile armies armies meet,
    O'ercome with fire and flame.
The sound is travelling through the earth,
    As fast as time can fly,
" Whoever takes the sword of war
    Shall fall himself thereby."

O ye who fan the fires of strife,
    And thicken human gloom,
Hear what the awful Judge proclaims;
    Blush at His words of doom.
Away, away with battle ships,
    Let peaceful pennons fly,
For he who takes the sword of war
    Shall fall himself thereby.

BEN FOREST AND JACK.

Ben Forest faced Jack plump in the long street,
With no room to sidle, and so they must meet.
They hugged an old grudge, like a miser his bags,
So Jack knocked Ben Forest down flat on the flags.

What a chance for a battle !   He rose from the stones,
Looked fiercely around as he felt his sore bones,
Then lost all excitement, gazed sadly on Jack,
Held his hand out in friendship, but never struck
    back.

This ended the contest.　But if in the fray
They had battered and bitten, like tigers at bay,
Oh how would have widened the chasm of dread,
Strong limbs have been twisted, and blood have been
　　　shed !

And think we of One, without blemish or stain,
Who, when they reviled Him, reviled not again.
They were friends ever after, Ben Forest and Jack,
And it all hinged on this—HE NEVER STRUCK BACK.

THE REIGN OF ENDLESS PEACE IS NEAR.

THE reign of endless Peace is near,
Away, away with sword and spear,
Let needle-guns and cannon lie
In foul neglect beneath the sky,
Or go to aid the wondrous rail,
Or iron ships before the gale.

Along the edges of the moor,
Through vines which shade the rustic door,
By temples old, o'er forest-sod,
Where red men meet to worship God,
The morn of Peace, in beauty bland,
Is breaking o'er the gladdened land.

The rich and poor secure shall dwell,
Unguarded then by ship or shell;
The rose and olive fill the glade,
The latest warrior sheath his blade,
Sweet Peace its living power attest,
And earth repose in perfect rest.

THE CRUISE OF THE CUTTER.

'he breeze bore her landward, the town was in sight,
'he moon o'er the waters was shedding her light :
'hey slackened their course, swerved round, and let go
. broadside of canister full on the foe.

'o answer ! no answer ! The anchor is cast,
.nd the topsails fall heavily on the high mast,
he boats are let down, and that war-working host
oon march with their butcher-blades over the coast.

hey enter the gates—not a warrior was there,
'ot a note of the trumpet bestirred the still air.
hey fought not, because there was no one to fight,
o back to the cutter they hastened that night.

'orget not the moral : let simple things speak ;
he stronger are sometimes relieved by the weak.
he sword and the spear would soon vanish from
    sight,
nd turn into shares, WERE THERE NO ONE TO FIGHT.

THE SOLDIER'S FATHER.

" LEAD Boxer to the stable, boy,
    We'll plough no more to-day :
And, Abel, see you give the beast
    A feed of corn and hay.

I must ride off this afternoon,
   As fast as we can go,
And get, within the market town,
   A doctor for our Joe.

" He left us when the elm was green,
   And corn was in the ear,
For lands where warriors walked the woods,
   And watched the passes drear.
Instead of peace, he bore a sword,
   Instead of meekness, might.
And in the soldier's coat of red
   He trampled on the right.

" His regiment was overpowered,
   And many men were slain :
For two long days, with shattered limbs,
   Joe lay upon the plain.
They brought him to his mother's home,
   A feeble, broken thing ;
So I must to the market town,
   And our good doctor bring.

" Men praise the mighty god of War,
   The demon-king of old,
And strive to hide his horrid rents,
   And gild his car with gold :
But sin has not in all its train,
   From the forlorn abyss,
Among the stricken tribes of earth,
   A greater curse than this."

THROUGH THE WOODS, AT CLOSE OF DAY.

Through the woods, at close of day,
Came an old man worn and gray,
And he sang with native art,
" Come, sweet Peace, and never depart."

Clear the echo rose and fell,
Over the dingle, and over the dell,
Over the moor, and over the mart,
" Come, sweet Peace, and never depart."

And the ploughman on the lea,
And the woodman 'neath the tree,
Caught the strain with glowing heart,
" Come, sweet Peace, and never depart."

Children sang where daisies grow,
Men whose hair was white as snow,
Duke, and driver by his cart,
" Come, sweet Peace, and never depart."

Thus the song that old man sang,
Through the gladdened nations rang,
Till the demon of War did start,
" Come, sweet Peace, and never depart."

OLD JOHN.

" We'll keep the kettle boiling, John,
   Perhaps our boy will come :
What gathering darkness has been ours
   Since first he left his home !
Heap up another lot of pine :
   Did not the letter say
That he would leave the hospital
   And be at home to-day ? "

The old man shook his locks of snow,
   And bowed his reverend head,
And, sitting in his own arm chair,
   He very slowly said, —
" Mishaps attend the soldier's life,
   And weariness and pain,
And much that offers fair is false ;
   So let us wait, dear Jane.

" I had a vision yester-eve,
   Of blossoms white and rare,
A little child the lion led,
   The wolf and lamb were there :
No tent of war was on the plain,
   The sounds of strife did cease,
And through the air an angel sang,
   ' It is the reign of Peace.'

" This blessed time will surely come;
    I pray for its advance,
When men shall not each other slay,
    With sabre, shot, or lance.
Our boy henceforth shall stay at home,
    And use the sword no more :
I hear a footstep in the lane;
    Hark ! hark ! he's at the door."

JOAN JAKES.

JOAN JAKES with her neddy, through dingle and dell,
Came into the market fresh cockles to sell.
Her cottage at Durgan was standing alone,
And none wore a bonnet old-fashioned like Joan.

One day, in a narrow lane near the old mill,
She talked to her neddy when climbing up hill :
" On earth we are lonely as lonely can be,
For there's nobody now but neddy and me.

" The war-trumpet sounded, and at the shrill call,
My son rushed to battle, my eldest, my all !
My husband had long been engaged in the fray :
And Fred and his father both fell in one day.

" The news came like darkness when thunder is strong,
I fell on the hearth-stone the ashes among,
And when I awoke from the terrible fright,
My summer was winter, my noontide was night.

" In the glory of warfare, when lances are crost,
How oft is the WIDOW forgotten and lost!
Gee, neddy, step faster, I'll trudge by thy side,
For we must reach Durgan before the next tide."

MATTY MASON.

" Who is this coming, Polly,
    Just down by Stennack stile ?
Treslothan lies beside him,
    Where yellow cowslips smile.
He's lingering near the ruin,
    By Matty Mason's tree ;
Perhaps it is her Jacob,
    Returning from the sea ?

" Rise up and call him, Polly,
    I always liked the lad ;
He has an honest visage,
    Although a little sad.
See, now, he takes his kerchief
    To wipe the falling tear.
The love of home increaseth
    With every passing year."

Then Jacob came to greet them,
    And heard with sobs of woe,
How in the village churchyard
    His mother slumbered low.

When he was soldiering fiercely,
 She died beside the tree,
Within her ruined cottage :
 " I've done with war," said he.

LIVE IN PEACE.

A LITTLE stream went flowing by,
Where vales were green, where hills were high,
And as it murmured on its way,
At eve and morn it seemed to say,
Still travelling downward to the sea,
" O, live in peace, where'er you be."

The pretty fishes 'neath the wave,
That hide in many a quiet cave,
The bees and flies that sport their hours
Around the lovely ferns and flowers,
Are ever whispering full and free,
" O, live in peace, where'er you be."

The rushy vale, the mountain brown,
The swallow wheeling o'er the down,
The solemn tarn, the echoing moor,
The boulders on the great sea shore,
All whisper, where the echoes flee,
" O, live in peace, where'er you be."

And there's a mystery on the height,
Which fills with sound the listening Night,
And in the bosom of the dell;
Who listens oft will hear it well,
The burden of the land and sea,—
" O, live in peace, where'er you be."

ROB ROOD.

At Lizard, by the Lion's Den,
    Rob left his youthful wife,
And donned the soldier's uniform,
    And rushed into the strife.
He vainly thought to gain renown,
    But lost his limbs and health,
And back at last he feebly came,
    A crutch his only wealth.

He gained a gentle eminence,
    From city-home aloof,
And saw the curling smoke ascend
    Beyond his cottage roof.
The milkmaid caroled on the mead,
    The lark was in the skies,
The ploughboy whistled by his team,
    And tears came in his eyes.

With his one hand he waved his cap,
    As on his crutch he leant,
To Susan standing by the door,
    And shouted as he went.

She held her smiling babe aloft,
   Who seemed her bliss to share,
So that the honeysuckles kissed
   His soft and shining hair.

He crossed the village bridge at last,
   And hobbled o'er the green,
And felt his own dear Susan's kiss
   The elder-brakes between :
Then sat within his humble home,
   With baby on his knee :
" O, wife, the sinful sword of War
   Is red with guilt," said he.

THE WHITE SHIP.

CAME a white ship o'er the sea,
Very white and fair was she,
With slender mast, and sails of snow,
Gliding over the waves below.

Not a gun, or pike, or sword,
Or bearded spearman was aboard ;
And Bible-texts the shrouds did show,
Gliding over the waves below.

There fairest damsels sweetly sang,
And viols thrilled, and trumpets rang ;
" 'Tis peace, 'tis peace, where'er we go,
Gliding over the waves below."

C

The echo rose from the peopled strand,
And quickly spread from land to land,
" 'Tis peace, 'tis peace, where'er we go,
Gliding over the waves below."

From old and young, from down and dell,
The conquering music rose and fell,
" 'Tis peace, 'tis peace, where'er we go,
Gliding over the waves below."

ISAAC ISLE.

'Twas Ember Week, and the lengthening light
Grew more and more on Boulder Height,
When Isaac Isle and his good wife Joan
Sat near the brands on the wide hearthstone,
Their glasses in their sheath-homes lay,
And Isaac Isle to his wife did say:

" The ends of the days are stretching, Joan;
I can see from here the Druid Stone.
Pull back the blind some inches more,
We need no candle yet, I'm sure,
And what a blessing again to be,
In a few weeks more, from lighting free!"

Just then as the brands a-flame did roar,
A tall thin man came in at the door;
On a crutch he leant, with a trembling gait,
Which seemed to cripple beneath his weight:
And he stood stock-still at his father's moan:
" 'Tis Tommy come back from the wars," cried Joan.

THE ORPHANS.

" O, WAIT a little, Lucy,
    The moon is o'er the lake,
Perhaps our dearest mother
    May very soon awake.
I never saw her sleeping
    So peacefully as now,
Or witnessed such a paleness
    Upon her cheek and brow.

" Has she not suffered hunger,
    And weariness and pain,
With longings that our father
    Would come to us again ?
Let's wait a little longer,
    Perhaps he may be here,
To comfort us in sorrow,
    And kiss away the tear."

The moon went down in silence,
    And yet no father came,
And day by day they waited,
    And it was still the same.
Alas ! their soldier-parent
    Will never see them more,
Down-trodden in the battle,
    With garments rolled in gore.

A VISION.

WHERE the woodbine and whortle arose,
   And held their sweet cups to the sun,
I sat in a dingle of rose
   When an evening of June had begun :
And far o'er the rock-covered wold,
   Where the, glory of sunset did lie
In currents of crimson and gold,
   A vision arose on mine eye :

A country of meadow and stream,
   With valleys of palm-tree and vine,
Where corn in its richness did gleam,
   And fattened the beautiful kine ;
The ploughman was on the wide mead,
   The milkmaid was under the tree,
The shepherd was tuning his reed
   Afar on the bountiful lea.

Here Peace, in a halo of light,
   Her sway o'er the populace spread :
No clamour arose on the night,
   No cry of the orphan for bread.
The sword and the battle-axe then
   Were changed to the glittering share,
And songs from the bosoms of men
   Swelled on the millennium air.

No brother chased brother to death,
    No master did fetter the slave,
No chief-trump received the warm breath,
    O, War had gone down to his grave.
And over the nations a joy,
    Ecstatic, fresh honours did win,
Which rifles would never destroy:
    The kingdom of Love had set in.

THE CHILD'S PRAYER.

No sound, no sound from bower or brake!
The crimson light was on the lake,
When a child prayed thus in her hamlet home,
" O, Father above, let Thy kingdom come!"

The eve-star glimmered above the pines,
And the sparrow had nestled among the vines,
As that child prayed soft in her dearest home,
" O, Father above, let Thy kingdom come!"

The moonlight stole through the Gothic panes,
And the bats were out in the woodbine lanes,
And prayed she thus in her quiet home,
" O, Father above, let Thy kingdom come!"

The dew came down in the floweret's cup,
And the leaves of the rose-tree drank it up,
And He heard her prayer in His highest home,
" O, Father above, let Thy kingdom come!"

The sound went forth from rill to rill,
From glade to glade, from hill to hill,
From town to town, from home to home,
" O, Father above, let Thy kingdom come!"

And the warrior's club became a flail,
And the spear was changed to the iron rail,
And Peace-strains rose from every home,
" O, Father above, let Thy kingdom come!"

ANNIE AND AMOS.

Adown to the well walked Annie,
    Humming a pastoral lay,
Thinking of one who had left her,
    Over the hills and away.
Whom should she see but a soldier,
    Looking so weary and worn ;
On the moss seat he was sitting,
    Under the favourite thorn.

He had deep scars on his forehead,
    He had deep scars on his breast,
And strikingly pale were his features,
    As if he were longing for rest.
He rose when she came to the fountain,
    And asked her to give him to drink,
And while he was holding the pitcher,
    She thought the poor fellow would sink.

At last their eyes met in the hollow :
　　The soldier gazed sadly, and sighed,
Whilst Annie her white arms uplifted,
　　" 'Tis Amos! 'tis Amos!" she cried.
And now in the cot of his father,
　　He trails his crushed foot on the floor,
And knows that for life he's a cripple,
　　Whilst Annie peeps in at the door.

THE SAD LETTER.

" READ out the letter, Susan :
　　Where did our Robert fall?
Was it by shell, or splinter,
　　Was it by blade, or ball ?
I in my chair will listen,
　　Beside the kindling brand,
My feet upon the fender,
　　My head upon my hand."

Then Susan read the letter,
　　Which from the captain came,
From side to side, all over,
　　By the pine branch's flame.
Upon a stormy rampart,
　　One noisy battle-day,
When blood was shed like water,
　　His life was blown away.

The old man moaned in spirit,
　　Like wind among the waves ;
And Susan's heart in fervour
　　Arose to Him who saves.
But no one knows the anguish,
　　The bitter cup of life,
Which that sad letter carried
　　To Robert and his wife.

LUCY LOO.

In a vale of withs, where the brooks were freed,
A cottage stood with its roof of reed :
'Neath the woodbine porch sang Lucy Loo,
While the gentle swallows around her flew,
And the redbreast listened on the latch,
And the sparrows looked down from the shaven thatch.

" I hear a voice in the rushes green,
I hear a voice in the rose's sheen,
I hear a voice in the waters' glide,
I hear a voice from the thicket's side,
That War shall soon in his grave-shroud lie,
And Peace-flowers bloom 'neath every sky.

" I hear a voice in the tinkling streams,
I hear a voice in my sweetest dreams,
I hear a voice at the vesper hour,
When the dew is cheering the forest flower,
And the lonely moon is mounting high,
That War shall soon in his grave-shroud lie.

" I hear a voice at evening prayer,
When wings of angels stir the air,
And silence filleth the listening dells,
And the sea-waves murmur among the shells,—
The echo of Him who fills the sky,—
That War shall soon in his grave-shroud lie."

THE LAME SCHOOLMASTER.

WHERE four roads met in quaintness
   Upon the hedgeless moor,
A lame old man instructed
   The children of the poor.
And, hanging in his school-room,
   Was many a curious board,—
" Why cannot wrongs be settled
   Without the flashing sword ?"

'Tis said, by those who knew him,
   That stripes were his disdain ;
He never beat a pupil,
   He never used a cane.
Yet rich became his scholars
   From Wisdom's golden hoard :
Why cannot wrongs be settled
   Without the flashing sword ?

And still the utmost order
   Prevailed throughout the place ;
He had some word of comfort
   To cheer the rising race :

And sang they morn and even,
    How Peace should be restored,
And every wrong be settled
    Without the flashing sword.

Forth went that old man's pupils
    Along their several ways,
With Peace-stars on their banners,
    Throughout the after days.
Each strove for arbitration,
    Of which we are assured,
When wrongs shall all be settled
    Without the flashing sword.

THE TRAVELLER.

A TRAVELLER reached a rustic town,
Just as the sun was sinking down,
And this his utterance, calm and clear,—
" The seeds of Peace I scatter here."

The plants grew on in light and dark,
And o'er them sweetly sang the lark :
Revived with dew, and sun, and shower,
They grew in beauty hour by hour.

And strife and discord left the hearth,
Where love and gentleness had birth,
And proud Oppression's reign was o'er,
And blows and bruises were no more.

And onward passed that ancient man,
From hill to hill, from clan to clan,
Scattering the seed with liberal hand,
Till Peace-flowers filled the lovely land.

WILLIE AND MEG.

MEG took her pitcher to the dell,
    Where ferns like fairies stood,
And then well-pleased she viewed herself
    Reflected in the flood ;
And thought of one, in soldier-vest,
    Who bade her hope and wait,
And when the corn was in the stack,
    She should be Willie's mate.

But she had waited wearily,
    The corn was threshed and sold,
And yet he knocked not at her door,
    Beside the shepherd's fold.
" He may be wounded in the fight,
    Or is he dead," thought she,
" And lying where the warriors fell ?
    For false he cannot be."

She heard a rustling in the grass,
    Upon the summer air,
And, looking round, how struck was she,
    For Willie's self was there !

And soon his arms were round her thrown,
  In love's untold embrace,
Her name upon his truthful lips,
  His kiss upon her face.

" O, Meg, I've seen enough," said he,
  " In camp and tented field,
Where many a warrior slept in death,
  Upon his broken shield.
'Tis wrong, 'tis wrong: I'll fight no more,
  Nor follow in the van,
Nor lift my arm in battle-work
  Against my fellow-man.

" Within yon cottage by the brook,
  We'll live among the flowers,
And Peace shall be our pleasant guest,
  And Nature's book be ours.
Cheer up, cheer up, my little Meg,
  My all to thee I bring ;
Before another month is past
  Our wedding bells shall ring."

OLD ABEL.

IN his cot where the Nine Maidens stand on the moor,
Old Abel sat down to his fire on the floor :
Said he, as the wood on the hearthstone did crack,
" I'd give my new buckles if Bobby were back."

Then Abel took down an old book from the shelf,
Where the print was quite large, which he kept for
      himself;
But his vision grew dim, and he stammered, " Alack!
I'd give my new buckles if Bobby were back."

So he put on his spectacles, turned the leaves o'er,
Threw on a fresh branch, and attempted once more,
But almost sobbed out, as the letters grew black,
" I'd give my new buckles if Bobby were back."

Then he sat in his chair, with his head on his hand,
And talked to himself, with his eyes on the brand,
" Ah! War leaves disaster and wrong in his track:
I'd give my new buckles if Bobby were back."

NED NORRIS.

NED NORRIS on the village green
    Was begging of the crowd;
His clothes were poor, his hair was thin,
    His frame with age was bowed,
And he looked as if his life had been
    For ever under a cloud.

He served his Queen on sea and land,
    Through many a long campaign;
He suffered where the rocks were rude,
    He suffered on the main,
And twice he felt the lance's point,
    And lay among the slain.

When he came home, his wife was dead,
　His children were no more,
Their graves were by the churchyard wall,
　Where sleep the village poor;
And so Ned Norris turned away,
　And begged from door to door.

He sometimes plays a violin;
　The tunes are sad and slow.
A grave will soon be made for him
　Beneath the hawthorn low.
Alas! that War should so much swell
　The tide of human woe.

BENNY BOND.

THERE came a gay sergeant to Benny Bond's door,
With scarlet and ribbon just half covered o'er,
And he told such a tale of the soldier's employ,
That his over-drawn speeches entrapped the poor boy.

Benny went off to fight with the Chinamen first,
Where he suffered from hunger, and suffered from thirst;
A leg was shot off in the midst of the fray,
And a sword-thrust he had in a desperate way.

He came home at last, when the fighting was o'er,
And knocked with his stick on his own mother's door:
But she did not know him, so sad and so pale,
Nor yet his dear Susan who lived in the vale.

His old father cried when he saw his own son
Come back to the village thus wrecked and undone.
Full soon in the workhouse he lay down to die,
And now in the grave of a pauper doth lie.

THE FARMER.

No one could stop the farmer :
   He buckled on his sword,
Brought out his snowy charger,
   And crossed the noisy ford ;
Then to his little sister,
   Within the lattice light,
He waved his hand at parting,
   And dashed into the fight.

No one could stop the farmer :
   He rode where swords were crossed,
And men of giant stature
   Were wildly hewn and lost.
Blood soaked the ground like water,
   And in red brooklets ran,
And groans arose in anguish
   From dying beast and man.

No one could stop the farmer :
   He passed where sons were slain,
And hoary-headed fathers
   Lay hacked upon the plain.

Blades fell with awful clangour,
     Which heads and helmets broke,
And Carnage sat in terror
     Upon his throne of smoke.

No one could stop the farmer :
     He swept through woods of spears,
With the sharp hiss of bullets,
     And steel-points in his ears :
On, on with headlong gallop
     Into the awful night,
Whence he returneth never
     Upon his charger white.

WILL WARD.

Will Ward passed by the farm-yard gate,
     His arm was in a sling,
He had been soldiering in the ranks,
     By order of the king.
They said 'twas noble thus to wear
     The coat of crimson hue,
And learn to shoot his fellow-men,
     And Will believed it true.

So off he went to fight the French,
     Equipped from head to heel,
With knapsack on his shoulder strapped,
     Bright musket and sharp steel.

And as he passed the holly-fence,
    The old thatched barn in sight,
He heard his father at the plough
    Say, " Why do Christians fight?"

The cannon roars, the war-steed moans,
    The hissing bullet rends,
And Will came back with broken limbs—
    A burden on his friends.
And, hobbling down the garden walk,
    Where roses blossomed bright,
He heard his father at the door
    Say, " Why do Christians fight ?"

His sorrowing mother dressed his wounds ;
    And Mary came to see,
Who with her thrifty parents dwelt
    Beside the shepherd's tree.
And oft the old man bent his head
    When Willie was in sight,
As if he spoke to one unseen,
    " No, Christians cannot fight."

THE DYING DRUMMER BOY.

On the crushed grass lay a drummer,
    A lad of just fifteen,
Whose life was ebbing slowly,
    Two dead war-steeds between :

D

And thus he spake in anguish,
   With utterance sad and slow :
" Do not our sainted kindred
   Still watch us here below ?

",Last night I thought my mother
   Came passing by that tree,
And bent and kissed my forehead
   As sweetly as could be;
Then slowly she ascended
   Beyond our sinful globe,
And in the hush of midnight
   I heard her snowy robe.

" O for a little water !
   I'm thirsty, and would drink.
I see a host of angels
   Upon the river's brink.
Pray beat my own drum o'er me,
   'Twill give my spirit joy
When I am laid to slumber."
   So died the drummer boy.

MILL MADO.

WHERE willows waved, and poplars tall,
Below a foaming waterfall,
Mill Mado, in a tattered frock,
Sat on the fragment of a rock,

Where snowdrops in the hollows gleam,
And thus she sorrowed to the stream:

" Flow on, flow on ! I'm lonely here,
No mother now to wipe the tear,
No father to embrace his Mill,
To kiss my cheek, and hush me still !
O, sword and spear, and flame and fire,
Destroyed my mother, home, and sire.

" How happy there we once did dwell,
Contented in our humble cell,
From morning dawn to evening's close,
Until the roar of War arose,
Whose echoes smote me on the wild,
And I am now an orphan child.

" Where shall I go my cup to fill ?
There's no one now to care for Mill.
But God, who dwells above the sky,
Will surely hear me when I cry,
And my first prayer to Him shall be
That warfare from the world may flee."

And then she sat in perfect ease,
Her head drooped gently on her knees,
The gathered snowdrops from her hand
Fell scattered on the mossy land,
And angels down the burning west,
Descending, took her home to rest.

CRIPPLED WILLIE.

" Who lives in that house yonder,
   Where woodbines reach the eaves,
With one small diamond lattice,
   Where roses rest their leaves ?
Ten years ago last Easter
   I left my Fanny here,
When for the wars we parted,
   And both brushed off the tear.

" We promised to be faithful
   Whatever might betide,
And when the war was over,
   She should be Willie's bride.
She hung upon my shoulder
   When I was going away,
And kissed my face so fondly,
   I wished that I could stay.

" But I had long enlisted,
   And thus was forced to go,
And twenty times I watched her
   Along the uplands slow :
She waved her snowy 'kerchief
   Till it was lost to sight ;
A hundred times I saw it
   When in the fiercest fight.

" I think I'll ope the wicket
　　And hobble to the door,
And stand beneath the woodbine
　　A-knocking as of yore."
And soon he looked on Fanny—
　　Alas! another's bride :
And in a few weeks after
　　Poor crippled Willie died.

UNCLE JABEZ.

" COME in, Uncle Jabez, the settle
　　Awaiteth you in the old hall.
That very deep scar on your forehead
　　Was made by a rifleman's ball.
You have been in the wars, Uncle Jabez,
　　Where weakness is trodden by might,
And force is the hero in laurel,
　　And strength is the author of right.

" Come into the hall, Uncle Jabez,
　　And Peggy shall bring you some meat :
Do put your great crutch in the corner,
　　And rest on the fender your feet.
Your days with the match-lock are over,
　　Your country will need you no more,
And yet they have left you to wander
　　Forsaken, and homeless, and poor.

" Come into the hall, Uncle Jabez,
    That I may your kindness return :
You saved my life once on the beacon,
    When the thunder-god spoke in the fern.
And goodness comes back to the giver,
    Although it may seem to delay.
My home is your home, Uncle Jabez,
    And here you are welcome to stay."

The old man advanced at her bidding,
    And sat in the snug proffered place,
And 'twas seen that he oft used his 'kerchief
    To wipe the warm tears from his face.
And Peggy came in with the platter,
    And placed before Jabez his mess :
He smoothed down his hair, and said softly,
    " Thank God for a friend in distress !"

THE HARPER.

THE moon shone on the boulders
    Around the beacon's base,
And Silence 'mid the ivy
    Sat with a thoughtful face,
When by it sang a harper,
    Whose notes were sweet and clear—
" Lift up your heads, ye peoples,
    The reign of Peace is near."

The old rocks seemed to answer,
    As in their lairs they lay,

With moonbeams for their helmets,
　　Like warriors after fray :
The pines upon its summit
　　Awoke the joyous cheer—
" Lift up your heads, ye peoples,
　　The reign of Peace is near."

The wind that swept the heather
　　And shook the whortle-brake,
The mosses of the moorland,
　　The wavelets of the lake,
Joined the prophetic music
　　Which stirred the solemn mere—
" Lift up your heads, ye peoples,
　　The reign of Peace is near."

The moon went down, and morning
　　Broke o'er the misty hills,
Fierce sunlight flamed the forest,
　　And flashed the flowing rills :
Yet there that harper standeth,
　　And harpeth year by year—
" Lift up your heads, ye peoples,
　　The reign of Peace is near."

DAME DOLO.

By Mainporth Crag, where the breakers foam,
Dame Dolo dwelt in her boulder home ;
And she was aged, and worn, and weak,
And the furrows were deep on her brow and cheek.

Dame Dolo sat by her fire of peat,
And throbbed her heart in the smouldering heat;
The wind like a war-steed paced the Crag,
And smote the water, and lashed the flag.

" My bread is done," Dame Dolo said,
" My cans are empty, my silver fled;
But though no way just now I see,
My Father above will care for me."

A voice at the lattice aroused the Dame,
From a soldier-man footsore and lame.
With earnest eyes around looked he,
'Twas her own dear Jack from over the sea.

What his wallet held was mean and small,
Though it served till the generous rector's call;
But his broken health nought could restore,
Till by Mainporth Crag he was seen no more,

ALF ANDREWS.

Alf Andrews sat upon a stool
    Beside his father's feet,
A pale-faced gentle-looking boy,
    With scarce enough to eat:
And thus he spoke, with thoughtful eyes,
    And slowly raised his head,
" Why don't you be a soldier, dad,
    And wear a coat of red?"

" No, no, my son. You know the man
    We met the other day
Beside the pines upon the peak ?
    His arms were shot away.
For years he served on foreign fields,
    With cutlass, pike, and gun,
In cold and heat, in strife and gore,
    And this is all he won.

" I'd rather live where Peace-flowers grow,
    Apart from human strife,
And feebly aid my fellow-men
    Along the road of life,
Than wear a soldier's crimson badge,
    To gain the hero's name,
In polished brass, and printed books :
    Away with such a fame !

" The happiest man is he, my son,
    Who lifts the load of care,
Who takes his brother by the hand
    Along the desert bare ;
Who fills the orphan child with bread,
    The widow's heart with joy,
And smoothes the evening path of life :
    Be such an one, my boy."

DOLLY DUFF.

In a corner of the workhouse
   Poor Dolly Duff was laid,
And all the village knew her
   As the thatcher's only maid.
Her father from a ladder
   Was killed upon the ground ;
She never knew her mother,
   Who long ago was drowned.

Within a little cottage,
   Where a path is through the grass,
She lived for many summers
   A gentle, thriving lass,
Till Tommy Truck came whirling
   His ivory-headed cane,
And wooed the maid, then left her
   In sorrow and in pain ;

Left her to fight the stranger,
   The woolly-headed black,
In dells where roves the panther,
   And never more came back.
A missile from a savage
   Laid Tommy in the dust,
Where pikes were plied in plenty,
   With many an angry thrust.

When Dolly heard the tidings,
    It was as if a stone
Had struck her in the thunder
    And shattered every bone.
They took her to the workhouse,
    And here she sadly lies,
Not heeding day or darkness,
    With shadows in her eyes.

PETER PINE.

'Twas Christmas-tide and carol,
    The ice was on the vine,
When down the lane came, slowly,
    Dear little Peter Pine.
His cap was old and shabby,
    His hair did strangely flow,
His coat had wide rents in it,
    His toes were in the snow.

Nine years was he last birthday,
    And at a roadside door
He told his simple story,
    Which grieved the listener sore.
His father in the warfare
    Was shattered by a ball,
When marching on to conquer,
    As rose the trumpet's call.

His mother pined to hear it,
    Like floweret on the moor,
When sudden frosts come chilling,
    And rising tempests roar:
And day by day she wasted,
    Till all her strength had flown;
Then angels called her to them,
    Where hunger is unknown.

So now he was an orphan,
    Poor little Peter Pine:
For two days had he fasted,
    His pale face showed the brine.
And sang he in his sadness,
    " O, lady, give me bread,
O, lady, gentle lady,
    I wish that I were dead!"

The moon arose at midnight
    Upon the glittering snow,
And flung her robes of silver
    On hill and vale below.
But Death had claimed the orphan,
    At that brief day's decline,
As 'neath the squire's low laurel
    Lay little Peter Pine.

BET BANKS.

Slow tolled the bells from Budock tower
Upon Saint Swithin's early hour;
The sexton by a grave did stand,
With spade and mattock near his hand,
When o'er the stile the mourners pressed,
Bearing a maiden to her rest.

" Whose grave? whose grave?" at length I said
To this stern hider of the dead.
The old man raised his bended form,
Like oak-tree crippled with the storm,
Where heath is low, and moors are wide,
And thus in earnest tones replied:

" Bet died, sir, of a broken heart:
Nay, thoughtful master, do not start.
Her lover left his cottage roof,
And fell beneath the charger's hoof,
Where guns did roar, and steel did ring:
O, War, sir, is a murderous thing.

" News reached our village when the eaves
Were hidden with the young grape-leaves;
And from that hour Bet felt a pain,
And never, never smiled again.
Let painters gild, and poets sing,
But War, sir, is a murderous thing."

DANIEL DEE.

A stone house on a common
　　Is standing by the sea,
And in this lonely dwelling
　　Resideth Daniel Dee.
One arm below the shoulder
　　Was severed with the sword,
When all King George's shooters
　　And spearmen were aboard.

Old Daniel Dee was helmsman,
　　And, falling on the deck,
They pitched him o'er the gunwale,
　　Which nearly broke his neck.
He floundered in the water,
　　Expecting soon to die,
Until a great wave left him
　　Upon the shingles dry.

He shook his well arm at.them,
　　Then hurried on his way :
But he was never cheerful
　　Or hopeful from that day.
So to this rocky dwelling
　　Retreated Daniel Dee,
To watch the swelling waters
　　Upon the changing sea.

And here he liveth lonely,
    And seldom doth rejoice ;
And oft at morn and even
    He lifteth up his voice,—
" The dreadful curse of curses,
    Whose night-fires gleam afar,
The monster of all monsters,
    Is rude red-handed War."

THE TWO SISTERS.

By Cuckoo Mills, where the waters glide,
Two sisters dwelt near the streamlet's side.
Their little window, clear as day,
Looked out on Swanpool's royal bay,
And as the sun's last rays were lent,
Thus talked they as their needles went :

" The sea may rise, the sea may roar,
Stitch, stitch we go for evermore ;
Our hands may ache, our hearts may sink,
And the vine-leaves watch us as they wink,
The winds may rest, or the winds may blow,
Yet stitch, stitch, stitch our needles go.

" Our only brother, our staff and stay,
Became a soldier last bright May.
He bullet-fell in the long campaign,
And his grave is washed with the Winter rain.
Were Willie here it would not be so,
Nor stitch, stitch, stitch our needles go."

LILA'S TALE.

'Twas hay-time on the Barton,
    The rake was in the grass,
And cheerful carols floated
    From many a lad and lass:
And sweetly down the dingle
    Was borne the pleasant tune,
Among the early woodbine
    And briony of June.

A mother and her daughter
    Came through the hay-field gate,
And dark distress and anguish
    Upon their visage sate.
The mother's cheeks were hollow,
    The maiden's face was pale,
And sad the hay-folks listened
    To little Lila's tale.

" Our supper meal was ended,
    And I my verse had read,
And told my ' Gentle Jesus,'
    Before I went to bed.
Then came the noisy clatter
    Of hoof, and spear, and men,
The door was burst and broken,
    And O how dreadful then !

" The soldiers killed my father,
    And with a cruel blow—
I fainted when they gave it—
    They laid my mother low.
And when again I wakened
    To consciousness at last,
Beneath the stars of midnight
    Our house was burning fast.

" The dreadful light it reddened,
    Illumined all the land;
But I rejoiced with weeping
    To feel my mother's hand.
And ever since we've wandered
    Away, and still away,
With little rest at night-time,
    With little food by day."

The sorrowing hay-folks fed them,
    And watched them up the hill,
Beyond the foaming river
    Which turned the lonely mill.
Away, away they travelled,
    Sojourning evermore.
O, when will War, the woeful,
    Be thrust from every shore!

THE GUNNER.

THROUGH the fields a gunner came,
Somewhat scarred, and somewhat lame :
Spoke he under a chestnut tree,
" This is the home of Molly and me.

" Day by day, as the battle roared,
Fed with famine, and fire, and sword,
Ever I saw it under the tree :
This is the home of Molly and me.

" In the fierceness of the fight,
Firing left, and firing right,
Up it rose like a vision free :
This is the home of Molly and me.

" Up the hill, and down the glade,
Where I've travelled, where I've strayed,
Nought is half so fair to see
As the home of Molly and me.

" Things will alter by and bye ;
Kings themselves should fight, say I.
Rest thee, soldier, under the tree :
This is the home of Molly and me."

WANA WERTHER.

"Sit down, my loves, to supper,"
　　Poor Wana Werther said,
"And let me give you quickly
　　The last dry crust of bread.
I wonder why your father
　　Should thus so long remain,
Where Havoc's arm is gory
　　Upon the dreadful plain.

"I'll take the road to Mawnan,
　　And watch below the tower,
Should any boats be coming
　　At this clear moonlight hour.
O, when will Reuben meet me?
　　O, when will War be o'er?
Hark! hark! a boat's keel grateth
　　Upon the silent shore."

'Tis Reuben, yes, 'tis Reuben,
　　But O how changed is he!
One arm has been shot from him,
　　His leg beyond the knee;
A bandage round his forehead
　　Half hides a fearful scar.
O, Reuben, soldier Reuben,
　　Are these the fruits of War?

E 2

'Tis said that in the winter,
  When winds were on the wold,
They perished in their dwelling,
  Of hunger, pain, and cold.
And still a woman's wailing
  Is heard along the shore,—
" O, when will Reuben meet me ?
  O, when will War be o'er ?"

PHIL FLAG.

PHIL FLAG dwelt on a mossy ridge,
A field or two from Mylor Bridge ;
He owned a garden by the leas,
Where pears and apples decked the trees,
And none had fruit, on moor or hill,
Compared in any way with Phil.

And Flag an old boat-seat had he
Under an ancient cherry-tree,
Where the neighbours came in the fading light,
And told sad tales of fire and fight,
When men marched forth at the bugle's blast :
" But Peace," said he, " will come at last."

Phil Flag in the battle had lost an eye,
And his own left hand with the slain did lie,
An ear was lopped with a swordsman's skill ;
" O, brethren, do not fight," said Phil.
Now his ruined home, on the mossy ridge,
Is not to be found by Mylor Bridge.

AGNES ARROW.

Not far from Helford Passage,
    Just up a narrow lane,
Resided Agnes Arrow,
    A widow poor and plain.
Her only son had left her,
    The fighting-ranks to swell,
And rumour said he perished
    When England's foemen fell.

So Agnes in her cottage
    Lived near the southern shore ;
And thus one eve she murmured,—
    " 'Tis no use waiting more :
I thought, perhaps, he'd see me
    When the great war was done ;
Yet I am ever lonely,
    From setting sun to sun.

" 'Tis no use waiting longer :
    Yet hark ! there's some one near ;
A moving of the wicket
    Methinks I faintly hear."
And in another moment
    She felt her son's embrace,
And knew it was her Robby ;
    And praises shook the place.

Yet he was scarcely like him,
    Her beautiful, her brave.
She nursed him in her chamber
    With what the parish gave.
And when the moon was rising,
    The crippled soldier died :
And he and Agnes Arrow
    Are sleeping side by side.

THE SOLDIER'S WIFE.

" Still Eve cometh out of her chamber,
    With the dew shining bright in her hair.
And homeward the ploughman doth whistle,
    Half stript of his burden of care :
But, baby, thy father will never
    Return to his dwelling again,
Or kiss the bright face of his Timmy,
    For now he lies dead on the plain.

" He pressed us so warmly at parting,
    And bade us be cheerful and gay,
And when he came back from the battle,
    He'd never again go away.
But he fell, so the newspaper sayeth,
    When making a gallant attack.
Alas ! for his widow and orphan,
    Alone on a desolate track !

" Hush, baby! my tears have aroused thee ;
    The wind cometh down from the height ;
Strange fingers are moving the lattice,
    The mystical murmurs of night.
Thou sleepest ! I'll pray by thy cradle,
    Where lieth his last offered toy
Thy father brought home to his darling.
    O, be not a soldier, my boy !"

CAPTAIN FRANK.

It was when Flushing Ferry
    Was owned by Captain Frank,
He told his simple story,
    When sitting on a plank :
" I had the finest boy, sir,
    That ever stood on shore,
That ever swung in hammock,
    Or ever handled oar.

" He joined the iron squadron,
    When strife was raging high,
And shot and shell were flying,
    And smoke-clouds hid the sky.
He strove to save his captain
    From Mussulman and Turk,
Who with long knives and muskets
    Dashed through their butcher-work.

" But whilst humanely striving
　　To shield his wounded friend,
Ten spear-thrusts in the action
　　Brought Philip to his end.
We waited for the tidings
　　Each mail-boat might impart,
And when the letter reached us,
　　It broke his mother's heart.

" Should you pass by my cottage,
　　Beyond the shingles bare,
His books and early trinkets
　　Are safely treasured there.
Ah ! if the wars were over,
　　If sword and strife were done,
I still should have his mother,
　　I still should have my son."

ARCHIE ARDOE.

A cot there is at Perranporth,
　　Alone upon the sand,
And Archie Ardoe liveth there
　　On three small fields of land.
A sword is hanging in his room
　　Against the plastered wall,
And Archie tells this tale of it
　　Whenever strangers call.

" I once was placed as sentinel,
　　Beside a patch of vines ;
The moon was rising in the east,
　　And lighting up the pines,
When down the hill a horseman dashed,
　　And strove to run me through ;
I turned aside his awful thrust,
　　Which broke my sword in two.

" My mates were soon aroused to act,
　　And stem the tide of strife,
And many a cheery comrade fell,
　　Bereft of limb and life.
O ! what I've seen, and what I've heard
　　In that dread carnage there,
When all the whelps of War were loose,
　　I never can declare.

" Suffice it, that I left a foot
　　And finger on the field,
And, sick at heart, I turned away
　　The scythe of Peace to wield.
My broken blade I brought with me,
　　And hung it on the wall ;
And morn and eve I always pray
　　That cruel War may fall."

THE BENIGHTED HUSSAR.

'Twas when the gorse was golden,
  In fragrance on the moor,
An old benighted soldier
  Knocked at the shepherd's door.
They gave him kindly greeting,
  And offered him a seat ;
And he was shortly chatting
  Beside the smoking peat.

The shepherd's little daughter
  Soon hushed her simple lay,
And gazed upon the stranger
  With eyes of tenderest ray ;
Then rose, and whispered sweetly,
  As she before him stood—
" This is the man, dear father,
  Who saved me from the flood."

With tears the gladdened mother
  The old hussar addressed,—
" Right welcome art thou, soldier ;
  We'll feed thee with the best.
Lay down thy simple wallet,
  And take the table's end,
And we will shortly show thee
  How we can feast a friend."

The soldier ate in silence,
    Then spoke, and looked above :
" I've learnt this holy lesson—
    The loftiest power is love.
And he who feeds the hungry
    At Friendship's generous board,
Is greater than the warrior
    Who buckles on his sword."

NAT NARDIP.

Nat Nardip disobeyed his sire,
    Refused to reap and mow,
And more and more his pride increased,
    Till he away did go.
He wandered on from town to town,
    Oppressed with want and shame,
Until, through rags and emptiness,
    A soldier he became.

They marched him off to Britanny,
    Where youth and age were slain,
When Nat, disabled, was dismissed,
    And home he came again.
Gray Eve was musing in the withs,
    As he drew near the door,
And the last carol of the lark
    Was ringing on the moor.

He waited till the dusk increased ;
　And when 'twas growing late,
With trembling step, and rising fears,
　He oped the garden gate :
And through the window he espied
　His father in his nook,
His mother with her knitting-sheath,
　His sister at her book.

He raised his hand, and feebly gave
　A very low rat-tat,
When Jetty oped the door, and cried,
　" O, mother, 'tis our Nat !"
" Come in, come in," the old man called,
　" I pardon all thy strife :
The erring wanderer is returned ;
　Down with the trencher, wife."

JOEY AND HIS MOTHER.

" Is Joey's bed ready, Charlotte ?
　Smooth down the sheets of snow,
And ope the little lattice
　About half-way, or so ;
Then place some sprigs of myrtle,
　Fresh gathered from the stem,
Within a glass of water,
　And put a rose with them.

" I'll seek the curious cromlech,
   Where swallows love to play,
And watch along the willows,—
   Perhaps he'll come to-day."
And saying this, she hastened
   Along the rocky down,
And watched till twilight settled
   Upon the beacon brown.

And every day she gathered
   Fresh myrtle from the frame,
Then climbed the hill and waited,
   And yet he never came.
His bed was always ready,
   The pillows placed with care,
Awaiting soldier Joey,
   And yet he came not there.

The widow's hair grew snowy,
   As year succeeded year,
In patient expectation,
   With faith and hope sincere.
Through wind, and rain, and sunshine,
   Still watched the loving dame,
And waited for her Joey,
   And yet he never came.

MARTIN'S PORRINGER.

" Don't sell our Martin's porringer,
  Although of low estate,
But leave it on the dresser-shelf,
  Beside the pewter plate.
'Twas his when he long lessons said
  Beneath the school house tile,
And also when a youth he joined
  The army of the isle.

" A thousand memories come to me
  When I behold it there,—
How oft I've danced him on my knee,
  And half forgot my care !
Or led him forth among the flowers,
  O'er many a rustic stile,
And little thought my boy would join
  The army of the isle.

" How pleased was I at supper time
  To see him in his place,
And felt so happy that the tears
  Would trickle down my face.
I hoped he would have tilled the farm,
  And raised the clover-pile,
And never dreamt my boy would swell
  The army of the isle.

" Don't sell that simple porringer,
  'Tis everything to me,
Since my poor boy, with soldier hands,
  Was buried by the tree :
Full oft it lessens loneliness,
  Although I weep the while
For him who joined, misled by fame,
  The army of the isle.

THE WAKENING WIND.

CAME a wind from the farthest hills,
Giving a voice to the crystal rills :
" Earth below, and heaven above,
Teach us ever to live in love."

Through the forest rode the blast,
Shaking the cedars as it passed :
" Earth below, and heaven above,
Teach us ever to live in love."

Swept that wind through ocean's caves,
Sounding aloud on the lifted waves :
" Earth below, and heaven above,
Teach us ever to live in love."

The nations rose with a gladdened soul,
And threw their swords to the mining mole :
" Earth below, and heaven above,
Teach us ever to live in love."

And mother and child, to the farthest vale,
Rejoiced in the sound of that sweeping gale
" Earth below, and heaven above,
Teach us ever to live in love."

OLD REUBEN.

" Is the scythe ready, Simon ?
   Just put it on the stone,
That it may cut with keenness
   The clover fully grown.
I've had no other helper
   Since Charlie went to sea,
A-fighting in the frigate ;
   So come and mow with me.

" If peace were always practiced,
   Abroad and at the board,
We should not need the soldier,
   We should not need the sword.
More useful is the plougher,
   Within the rural glen,
And he who moweth clover,
   Than he who moweth men.

" Be this thy maxim, Simon,—
   That sword and spear shall cease,
And men of every colour
   Shall bind the sheaf of Peace.

Then trumps unheard by mortal
  Shall on the heights be blown,
And glow along the valleys
  A glory yet unknown.

" The time is speeding, Simon,
  When strength will yield to worth.
And the delicious olive
  Shall flourish o'er the earth.
Then charity shall conquer,
  As overcome it must,
And every battle-weapon
  Be buried in the dust."

The scythe was in the clover :
  Old Reuben's words were there,
They came with every rustle
  That laid the meadow bare ;
In Simon's ears they tingled,
  Like some angelic chord,
That charity should conquer,
  And not the lifted sword.

GRANNY LEE.

" How far is it to Falmouth Fort ?"
  Enquired old Granny Lee,
" I hear my soldier Sam is there,
  As ill as boy can be.

F

O soldier Sam ! O soldier Sam !
    Why did you go away,
When your own mother and your bride
    Implored you so to stay ?

" And why do nations practice strife,
    And do their neighbours ill,
When He who came to give us life
    Commands us not to kill ?
O soldier Sam ! O soldier Sam !
    Where can thy dwelling be ?
Thou canst not tell the sharp distress
    I have endured for thee."

Then up Pendennis height she passed,
    And o'er the drawbridge sped,
Where paced the silent sentinel
    With slow and measured tread.
She gained the outer barrack door,
    Beside the castle-keep,
Whose frowning batteries ever hold
    Strict watch upon the deep.

And soon the tidings reached her ears,
    And froze her where she stood,
That soldier Sam was in his grave,
    Beside the murmuring flood ;
And that he talked, as death came quick,
    Of how he longed to see
His wife of only fourteen days,
    And dear old Granny Lee.

THE LAST ATTACK.

THE lurid air with shocks was rent,
Arose one heavy, huge lament,
From shepherd's shed, and warrior's tent.

Great towers lay prostrate in the gloom,
With cities 'neath the foot of Doom,
And Mercy found on earth no room.

The widow wailed her husband dead,
The orphan died for lack of bread,
And love and charity were fled.

Gore dripped from peaks of frozen snow,
And stained the silent flowers below,
Wherever erring man could go.

The battered corpses rose in hills,
And blood rushed down in swollen rills,
And greatest he who greatest kills.

Then came a voice across the dark,
The steady gunner missed his mark,
And desperate swordsmen whispered, " Hark ! "

'Twas Peace with all her gentle train,
O'er every clan and clime to reign :
And swords were never raised again.

HURRAH FOR THE SHARE!

Hurrah for the share! the shining share!
Where the ploughman breathes the country air,
Where the daisy blooms by the granite cross,
And the snowdrop muses among the moss,
And the blue-bells hang in their arbours rare:
Hurrah! hurrah for the shining share!

Hurrah for the share! the shining share!
Which has nought of the soldier's borrowed glare:
No desperate deeds, with fire and shout,
No ransacked cities, no homes burnt out,
No states o'erturned, no lands laid bare,
Can ever be placed to the shining share.

Hurrah for the share! the shining share!
Which doth for the scythe and the flail prepare,
Which bringeth the loaf to the poor man's board,
And addeth its store to the prince's hoard.
Without it the shelf and the cupboard were bare,
Hurrah for the share! the shining share!

LETTY LORE.

" The way is lonely, Letty,
  The cold night-wind is high,
No star looks through the darkness,
  No moon is in the sky:

The great trees shake with watching,
  A sigh is on the snow,
And Letty Lore is weary :
  Ah! whither shall we go ?

" Dost hear the thunder, Letty,
  Along the northern height ?
The mountain-gods are angry
  For deeds of death to-night.
The household-head is smitten,
  The child an orphan made,
The peaceful wife a widow,
  To glut the soldier's trade.

" A light in yon small window
  Is shining through the gloom ;
We'll knock, and ask the cottar
  To give the houseless room."
And soon before the faggot
  They whispered in the heat,
While Goody fried the rasher,
  And brought the broken meat.

There are true hearts and tender
  In every Christian clan,
So that sometimes the stronger
  Assists the weaker man.
Nor is affection warmer,
  From farthest east to west,
Nor charity more lovely,
  Than in the peasant's breast.

RIMMER RICE.

OLD Rimmer's home, by Enys Wood,
In a sheltered vale of cowslips stood,
With Gothic porch, and oaken latch,
And woodbine climbing to the thatch :
With no companion but his dog,
Thus talked he by the beechen log :—

" Alone! alone! with the great wind high,
And ragged rents in the stormy sky !
With failing sight, and trembling hands,
And a loosening sense of the silver bands ;
Whilst on the shaken almond tree
The dry leaves rustle of dusk to be !

" First Frank went off to fight the foe :
His grave is green where the willows grow.
Then Tommy joined the spearing horde,
And died beneath the Moslem's sword.
Fell one by one, till all were slain,
And I'm alone with the wind and rain.

" For all mankind, how well, how well,
In love and lasting peace to dwell !
Then spear-trained armies were a sin,
Nor darts be hurled from kin to kin,
But wheat-ears hide the barrack-stone,
Nor Rimmer Rice be all alone."

WORKS BY THE SAME AUTHOR.

Superbly bound in antique cloth, gilt back and side,
Fcap. 8vo., 386 pages, price 6s.

Bulo: Reuben Ross: A Tale of the Manacles:
Hymn, Song and Story.

Elegant antique cloth, gilt back and stained edges,
Fcap. 8vo., 272 pages, price 5s.

Luda: a Lay of the Druids.
Hymns, Tales, Essays and Legends.

In superior crimson and green cloth, gilt edges, containing the
Shakspere Tercentenary Prize Poem. Fcap. 8vo., 5s.

Shakspere's Shrine: An Indian Story:
Essays and Poems.

Cloth, gilt edges, Fcap. 8vo., price 4s.

A Story of Carn Brea; Essays and Poems.

Cloth, gilt edges, price 4s.

The Mountain Prophet, The Mine, and other
Poems.

Cloth, gilt edges, price 3s. 6d.

The Land's End, Kynance Cove, and other
Poems.

Cloth, gilt edges, with lithographic frontispiece.
Second edition, price 4s.

Lays from the Mine, the Moor, and the Moun-
tain.

EXTRACTS FROM CRITIQUES.

From THE ATHENÆUM, *October 4th*, 1856.

" His writing to any other age would have been a marvel, and it is a phenomenon even in our own. Stirs the blood like wine, and fills us with a fuller strength."

From THE ATHENÆUM, *May 9th*, 1863.

" As a writer of verse, John Harris has earned a place by the side of Robert Bloomfield."

From THE ATHENÆUM, *December 12th*, 1868.

" A simple, natural poet, such as every race but too rarely produces, and of a kind which differs to the core from that of the sentimental and whining bards who so frequently publish what should be hidden. Mr. Harris was a Cornish miner, who has written verses which, compared with those that spring from some ardent claimants on the public purse, are as the wine of flowers to the stagnant water of a froggy pool."

From THE CRITIC, *October 1st*, 1856.

" Mr. Harris has the true instincts and perfect skill of the artist. (*February 19th*, 1859). Has not written in vain, if labour needed another gifted soul of song to dignify it."

From THE LONDON QUARTERLY REVIEW, *April*, 1867.

" A poet of no common gifts, and there is a ring of truth and genuineness in his works which convince us that he is an honest and worthy man."

From THE NEW BRITON JOURNAL (*America*).

" A man of whom Cornwall may well be proud. A true poet, who has written and published poems full of lyric beauty, and with all the pastoral freshness of a pure-hearted child of nature."

From THE LITERARY GAZETTE, *December 15th*, 1860.

" We do not hesitate to call John Harris, Cornish miner, one of the truest poets of our time."

From THE CHRISTIAN WITNESS.

" Mr. Harris is a man worthy to rank in the same class with Samuel Drew, and other gifted spirits that have derived their birth from Cornwall."

From the RIGHT REV. THE LORD BISHOP OF WINCHESTER *to* ROBERT ALEXANDER GRAY, ESQ.

" Will you, at my request, say for me a kind word to the author? All poetry whatsoever that reveals character is a gift to humanity."

From his Worship THE LORD MAYOR OF LONDON, *December 14th*, 1871.

" In compliance with the suggestion of my dear friend, R. A. Gray, Esq., I have had the pleasure of subscribing to your meritorious volume, which has afforded me much pleasure, and is highly esteemed by several of my friends to whom I have presented them. I trust you may be long spared to do much credit to your picturesque county, and to enrich the literature of the century.   I am, truly yours,
THOMAS DAKIN, *Lord Mayor of London*, 1871."

LONDON : HAMILTON, ADAMS AND CO.
FALMOUTH : THE AUTHOR.

NEW WORKS AND NEW EDITIONS

PUBLISHING BY

S. W. PARTRIDGE & CO.,

9, PATERNOSTER ROW, LONDON.

The City Temple: a Pulpit Register and a
Church Review; containing Chapters I. to XVII. of "Raven Digby."
By Joseph Parker, D.D. Demy 8vo, cloth, 6s.

The City Temple. Sermons Preached in
the Poultry Chapel, London, by Joseph Parker, D.D., 1870-71. New
Series, demy 8vo, cloth, 5s.

The Book of the Relevation of Jesus Christ.
Illustrated by a Diagram, with Explanatory Notes. By Rev. J. G.
Gregory, M.A., Author of "Earth's Eventide," &c. Demy fol., cloth, 5s.

Songs from the Woodlands; and other
Poems. By B. Gough, Author of "Lyra Sabbatica," "Kentish Lyrics,"
&c. With Frontispiece. Crown 8vo, cloth, 3s. 6d.

The Temperance Bible Commentary; giving
at One View, Version, Criticism, and Exposition, in regard to all
passages of Holy Writ bearing on "Wine" or "Strong Drink," or
illustrating the Principles of the Temperance Reformation. By F. R.
Lees, and Dawson Burns. Third Edition. Demy 8vo, cloth, 6s.

Beads Without a String; Brief Thoughts on
Many Subjects. By S. W. Partridge, Author of "Upward and
Onward," &c. Crown 8vo, cloth, 4s.; gilt, 5s; mor. 8s.

Gathered Grain: consisting of Select Ex-
tracts from the best Authors. New and Cheaper Edition. Crown 8vo,
cloth, 3s. 6d.

The "I Am's" of Christ: Thoughts on the
Lord's Attributes, as Unfolded by Himself. By A. S. Ormsby, Author
of "Heart Whispers," &c. Cloth, 2s.; cloth, gilt edges, 3s.

Messages from the Risen Saviour. For
Mothers' Meetings. By the Author of "Glimpses of Heaven," &c.
Fcap. 8vo, cloth, 1s. 6d.

The Parish Apprentice; or, John Winzer,
the North Devon Puritan. By Rev. S. Newnam. Second Edition.
With Frontispiece. Fcap. 8vo, cloth, 1s. 6d.

Autopædia; or, Instructions on Personal
Education. Designed for Young Men. By J. McCrie, D.D., Author
of "The Primal Dispensation," &c. Second Edition, enlarged. Demy
8vo, cloth, 7s. 6d.

The Two Babylons; or, the Papal Worship
proved to be the Worship of Nimrod and his Wife. With 61 Illustrations from Nineveh, Babylon, Egypt, Pompeii, &c. By the Rev. A.
Hislop, of East Free Church, Arbroath. Fourth Ed. Cr. 8vo, 7s. 6d.

The Tabernacle of Israel. Illustrated. By
H. W. Soltau. Eight Chromo-lithographic Plates. Imperial oblong
8vo, cloth, gilt edges, 16s.

Cottage Readings in Genesis. Second Edition.
By the Author of "Cottage Readings in Exodus." Crown 8vo, 5s.

Voices that are Near. A Book of Parables
for Young Folk. With Frontispiece. Fcap. 8vo, cloth, 2s. 6d.

Hymn-Writers and their Hymns. By Rev.
S. W. Christophers. Library Ed., 7s. 6d. New and Cheaper Ed., 3s. 6d.

What shall my Son be? Hints to Parents
on the Choice of a Profession or Trade, and Counsels to Young Men on
their entrance into Active Life. Illustrated by Anecdotes and Maxims
of Distinguished Men. Also, a Copious Appendix of Examination
Papers, and other Practical Information. By Francis Davenant, M A.
Crown 8vo, cloth, 7s. 6d.

The Peerage of Poverty ; or, Learners and
Workers in Fields, Farms, and Factories. By E. Paxton Hood, Author
of "Self Formation," "Blind Amos," &c. Demy 8vo, cloth, 7s. 6d.

Bye-path Meadow. By the same Author.
Coloured Frontispiece. Crown 8vo, cloth, 3s. 6d.

The Royal Merchant ; or, Events in the
Days of Sir Thomas Gresham, Knight, as narrated in the Diary of
Ernst Verner, whilom his Page and Secretary, during the Reigns of
Mary and Elizabeth. By W. H. G. Kingston, Esq., Author of "The
Martyr of Brentwood," &c. With Portrait. Crown 8vo, cloth, 6s. 6d.

Lectures on St. Paul's Epistle to the
Ephesians. By the Rev. William Graham, D.D., Bonn, Prussia, Author
of "On Spiritualising Scripture," &c. Crown 8vo, cloth, 7s. 6d.

The Jews ; their Past, Present, and Future :
Being a succinct History of God's Ancient People in all Ages; with the
Origin of the Talmud, and the Numbers of Jews in all Countries of the
World. By J. Alexander. Small 8vo, 2s. 6d.

Philip Moore, the Sculptor; or, Genius, Per-
severance, and Temperance. By the Author of "Lindsay Lee and his
Friends," &c. With Frontispiece. Fcap. 8vo, cloth, 2s. 6d.

Daybreak in Italy : a Tale of the Italian
Reformation. By E. Leslie. Coloured Frontispiece. Cloth, 3s. 6d.

Notes of Sermons of the late Rev. John
Offord, Minister of Palace Gardens Chapel, Kensington. 8vo, 3s. 6d.

A Reply to Cobbett's "History of the
Reformation in England and Ireland." Compiled and Edited by
Charles Hastings Collette. Demy 8vo, cloth, pp. 350. 5s.

The Gospel Treasury, and Practical Expo-

sition of the Harmony of the Four Evangelists. Compiled by R. Mimpriss. Library Edition. Large type, demy 4to, 1,100 pages. Fifth Thousand. Cloth, 16s.; half calf, 22s.; whole calf, 30s.—Crown 8vo edition, 950 pages. 27th Thousand. Cloth, 6s.; calf gilt, 8s. 6d.; morocco, 10s.

Mick Tracy, the Irish Scripture Reader.

With Engravings. Thirteenth Thousand. Crown 8vo, cloth, 3s. 6d.

Tim Doolan, the Irish Emigrant : being a

full and particular Account of his Reasons for Emigrating—His Passage across the Atlantic—His Arrival in New York—His brief Sojourn in the United States, and his further Emigration to Canada. By same Author. With Frontispiece. Second Edition. 3s. 6d.

The Pilgrim's Progress from this World to

That which is to Come. By John Bunyan. With Memoir by Rev. W. Landels, D.D. Fcap. 4to, printed in clear type, with 74 Coloured Engravings. Fourth thousand. Elegant cloth, 5s.

The Life of Jesus. For Young People.

By the Editor of "Kind Words." Profusely Illustrated with Original Engravings. Tenth Thousand. Crown 8vo, cloth, gilt edges, 5s.

The Great Antichrist: Who? When?

Where? A Contribution for Anxious Times. By Rev. W. J. Bolton, M.A., Author of Hulsean Prize Essay for 1852, &c. With Lithographic Frontispiece. Crown 8vo, cloth, 1s. 6d.

The Pastor's Wife : a Memoir of Mrs. Sher-

man, of Surrey Chapel. By her Husband. With Portrait. Thirteenth Thousand. Cloth, 3s. 6d.

The Road to Rome, via Oxford ; or, Ritu-

alism Identical with Romanism. By Rev. J. A. Wylie, LL.D., Author of "The Papacy," &c. Crown 8vo, cloth, 5s.

Blind Amos and His Velvet Principles ; or,

Proverbs and Parables for the Young Folk. By E. Paxton Hood. New Edition. Crown 8vo. Coloured Frontispiece and Title, 1s. 6d.

Anti-typical Parallels ; or, The Kingdom of

Israel and of Heaven. With Notes, Illustrations, and Maps of the Original Occupation of Palestine, and of the Millennial Kingdom. By Lieut.-General Goodwyn. Royal 8vo, cloth, 16s.

"The Crusher" and the Cross. A Narrative

of a Remarkable Conversion. By A. Fergusson, Author of "Life's Byways," &c. Crown 8vo, cloth, 2s. 6d.

St. Mary's Convent; or, Chapters in the

Life of a Nun. By the Author of "Thady D'Arcy," &c. 2s. 6d.

Counsels and Knowledge from the Words of
Truth. Second Edition. By Rev. F. Whitfield, M.A. Cr. 8vo, cl. 3s. 6d.

Spiritual Unfoldings from the Word of Life.
By the same Author. Second Edition. Crown 8vo, cloth, 3s. 6d.

The Word Unveiled. By the same Author.
Crown 8vo, cloth, 3s. 6d.

Gleanings from Scripture. By the same
Author. Third Edition. Crown 8vo, cloth, 3s. 6d.

Earth's Eventide, and the Bright Dawn of
the Eternal Day. By Rev. J. G. Gregory, M.A., Minister of Park
Chapel, Chelsea, late Rector of Ponchurch. Fourth Edition. 8vo, 4s. 6d.

Winnowed Grain ; or, Selections from the
Addresses of the Rev. J. Denham Smith. *Cheaper Edition.* Demy
16mo. Third Edition. Cloth, 1s. 6d.

Truth Better than Fiction; or, Interesting
Tales and Anecdotes for the Young. By Francesca H. Wilson. 1s. 6d.

The True Rights of Woman. By Fanny
Aikin-Kortright. Second Edition. Demy 8vo, 1s. 6d.

Our English Months; a Poem on the Seasons
in England. By S. W. Partridge. Crown 8vo, cloth, 6s.; gilt, 7s. 6d.;
morocco, 10s. 6d.

Upward and Onward ; a Thought Book for
the Threshold of Active Life. By the same Author. Ninth Thousand.
Crown 8vo, cloth, 4s. ; gilt, 5s. ; morocco, 8s.

BOOKS FOR THE TIMES.
Crown 8vo, cloth, 1s. each.

The Last Look; a Tale of the Spanish Inquisition. By
W. H. Kingston, Esq.

Count Ulrich of Lindburgh ; a Tale of the Reformation in
Germany. By the same.

The Martyr of Brentwood; or, 300 Years Ago. By same.

Margaret's Venture. By Author of "Jenny's Geranium."

The O'Tooles of Glen Imaal. By Rev. G. R. Wynne.

The Curate of West Norton. By the same.

The Converts of Kilbann : an Irish Story. By the same.

Henry Hilliard ; or, The Three College Friends.

Overton's Question, and What Came of It.

Carey Glynn; or, The Child Teacher. By Rev. Dr. Leask.

(Full Catalogues on application.)

LONDON: S. W. PARTRIDGE & Co., 9, PATERNOSTER ROW.

www.ingramcontent.com/pod-product-compliance
Lightning Source LLC
Chambersburg PA
CBHW020310090426
42735CB00009B/1294